CANDLE
Day by Day
Prayers

Presented to

....

By

....

On this day

....

**CANDLE
BOOKS**

Published by Candle Books
an imprint of
Lion Hudson plc
Wilkinson House, Jordan Hill Road,
Oxford OX2 8DR, England
www.lionhudson.com/candle

ISBN 978 1 78128 265 6

First edition 2016

Acknowledgments
Every effort has been made to trace and contact copyright owners. We apologize for any inadvertent omissions or errors.

All unattributed prayers by Tim Dowley are copyright Lion Hudson/Tim Dowley Associates Ltd

The following prayers are by (or adapted from prayers by) Claire Freedman: 7, 15, 123, 130, 160, 180, 185, 187, 198, 203, 219, 221, 227, 233, 234, 246, 258, 266, 272, 274, 313, 320, 325, 342, 343, 350, 352

Prayers by Karen Williamson and Claire Freedman are copyright © Lion Hudson/Tim Dowley Associates Ltd

The following extracts taken or adapted from The Book of Common Prayer, the rights in which are vested in the Crown, are reproduced by permission of the Crown's patentee, Cambridge University Press: 21, 41, 252, 349, and 361.

The Lord's Prayer (37) is adapted from the Holy Bible, New Living Translation, copyright © 1996, 2004, 2007 by Tyndale House Foundation. Used by permission of Tyndale House Publishers, Inc., Carol Stream, Illinois 60188. All rights reserved.

"Two little eyes to look to God" (186) copyright © Mr Ian Kerr

Scripture quotations marked CEV are taken or adapted from the Contemporary English Version copyright © 1991, 1992, 1995 by American Bible Society. Used by permission.

Scripture quotations marked NIV are taken from the Holy Bible, New International Version® NIV® Copyright © 1973, 1978, 1984 by Biblica, Inc.® Used by permission. All rights reserved worldwide. The "NIV" and "New International Version" are trademarks registered in the United States Patent and Trademark Office by Biblica, Inc.® Use of either trademark requires the permission of Biblica, Inc.®

Scripture quotations marked JB are taken or adapted from The Jerusalem Bible, published and copyright 1966, 1967 and 1968 by Darton, Longman & Todd Ltd and Doubleday and Co. Inc, and used by permission of the publishers.

Scripture quotations marked TLB are taken from The Living Bible copyright © 1971 by Tyndale House Foundation. Used by permission of Tyndale House Publishers Inc., Carol Stream, Illinois 60188. All rights reserved.

Scripture quotations marked GNB are taken from the Good News Bible © 1994 published by the Bible Societies/HarperCollins Publishers Ltd UK, Good News Bible © American Bible Society 1966, 1971, 1976, 1992.
Used with permission.

Scripture quotations marked NRSV are taken from the New Revised Standard Version Bible: Anglicized Edition, copyright © 1989, 1995 National Council of the Churches of Christ in the United States of America. Used by permission. All rights reserved.

A catalogue record for this book is available from the British Library

Printed and bound in Malaysia, March 2016, LH18

CANDLE
Day by Day
Prayers

compiled by Juliet David

illustrated by Jane Heyes

**CANDLE
BOOKS**

CONTENTS

Why Pray?

What is prayer?

Prayer is spending time with God. When we spend time with a friend, we often talk. Sometimes we just sit quietly together. Praying to God is being with a very special friend.

Who do we pray to?

We pray to God.
Sometimes we start as if we're talking to a very important person: 'O God.'
Sometimes we start as if we're starting a letter: 'Dear God.'
Sometimes we say 'O Lord' or 'Heavenly Father'.
When we pray we talk to God.

Do we have to say prayers out loud?

God is everywhere and he knows everything. So God can hear a prayer even if we just say it in our mind. When we are together, we often say our prayers out loud so others can join in.
God hears every kind of prayer – loud or silent.

Should we use special words when we pray?

God understands our prayers, whatever words we use.

Can we make up our own prayers?

Sometimes we use prayers that are written down. Sometimes we use our own words. We don't have to use clever words.
Sometimes we pray silently.
We pray whenever we talk to God from the heart.

Do we have to say 'amen' at the end of every prayer?

We often say 'amen' at the end of a prayer. It's an old way of saying 'may it be so'. We don't have to say it.
If one person says a prayer aloud, it's good to join in saying 'amen'.
We say 'amen' to show we mean our prayer.

Can we pray to Jesus?

Jesus is God's son. Some people find it helpful to pray to Jesus. They imagine talking to him.
When we pray, we often finish by saying 'in Jesus' name'.

Do we have to kneel to pray?

Some people kneel to pray.
Some stand up.
Some people hold their hands together.
Some hold their hands out – or up.
God hears us, however we are.

Do we have to go to church to pray?

When we go to church, we pray together. But we can also pray alone in our room. Jesus often went off alone to pray.
Prayer is not something to show off about – it's between you and God.

Is there a right time to pray?

We can pray when we wake up.
We can pray before eating.
We can pray before a journey.
Many people pray before they go to sleep.
We can pray to God any time.

If we ask God for things we want, will we get them?

God wants us to enjoy life. But best of all is being a close friend of God. When we pray, God helps us see what will make us truly happy. God wants to give us good things.

If God knows everything, why do we need to pray?

God already knows what we think and need and want.
But it's good to be friends of God. Praying helps us see things God's way.

Hooray for God!

1   Lord, I will praise your name
    because you are good.

Psalm 54:6 CEV

---

2   The lark's on the wing;
    The snail's on the thorn:
    God's in his heaven –
    All's right with the world!

Robert Browning (1812–89), English poet

---

3   Thank you for the sunshine bright,
    Thank you for the morning's light,
    Thank you for the rainy showers,
    Thank you for the fruit and flowers.
    Amen

Traditional

4   I will praise you, Lord, among the nations;
I will sing of you among the peoples.
For great is your love,
Reaching to the heavens;
Your faithfulness reaches to the skies.

Psalm 57:9–10 NIV

Hooray for
God!

5   Praise the Lord! The heaven adore him!
Praise him, angels in the height!
Sun and moon, rejoice before him!
Praise him, all the stars and light.

attributed to John Kempthorne (1775–1838), English clergyman

6   Sing joyfully to the Lord, all you lands;
Serve the Lord gladly;
Come before him with joyful songs.
Know that the Lord is God:
He made us; we are his.
We are the flock he cares for.
Give thanks to him.

after Psalm 100

7   Clap your hands and shout for joy,
    God loves every girl and boy.
    Praise God!

8   Dear Lord,
    I praise you
    because of the wonderful way
    you created me.

    based on Psalm 139:14 CEV

9   Oh give thanks unto the Lord,
    for he is good.
    For his mercy is forever.

    based on Psalm 106:1

10 God bless the field and bless the furrow,
    Stream and branch and rabbit burrow…
    Bless the minnow, bless the whale,
    Bless the rainbow and the hail…
    Bless the earth and bless the sea,
    God bless you and God bless me.

    Traditional

11 Dear Lord,
I love our world
Thank you for making it the way you did.

12 Hooray for God
in heaven above!

Mark 11:10 CEV

13 Lord God… you deserve to be praised
forever and ever.
Let everyone say, "Amen!
Shout praises to the Lord!"

Psalm 106:48 CEV

11

14 Praise the Lord! Praise the Lord!
Let the earth hear his voice!
Praise the Lord! Praise the Lord!
Let the people rejoice!

Oh, come to the Father
through Jesus the Son,
And give him the glory,
great things he has done.

Fanny J. Crosby (1820–1915)

---

15 Dear God,
Sometimes I don't talk to you
– but I know you're still there.
Thank you.
Amen

---

16 Praise him, praise him
Everybody praise him –
He is love, he is love.
Praise him, praise him,
Everybody praise him –
God is love, God is love!

Traditional

New Every Morning

17   As I wake today,

May the strength of God pilot me,

The power of God uphold me,

and the wisdom of God guide me.

after St Patrick, fifth-century missionary in Ireland

18   Now, before I run to play,

Let me not forget to pray

To God, who kept me through the night

And waked me with the morning light.

Help me, Lord, to love you more

Than I ever loved before;

In my work and in my play,

Please be with me through the day.

13

19   O Lord,

Let dawn bring news of your faithful love,

For I put my trust in you;

Show me the road I must travel

for you to relieve my heart.

Psalm 143:8 JB

20   For this new morning with its light,

Father, we thank you.

For rest and shelter of the night,

Father, we thank you.

For health and food, for love and friends,

For everything your goodness sends,

Father in heaven, we thank you.

Ralph Waldo Emerson (1803–82), American poet

21   O Heavenly Father,

In whom we live and move and have our being,

We humbly pray you so to guide us by your Holy Spirit,

That in all the cares and occupations of our daily life

We may not forget you,

But remember that we are always walking in your sight.

For your name's sake.

from *The Book of Common Prayer*

22   Thank you, God in heaven,
For a day begun.
Thank you for the breezes,
Thank you for the sun.

Traditional

23   Lord, please help me
as I start a new day.
And help my friends.
Amen

24   Each morning when I wake, I say,
"Take care of me, dear Lord, today."

25   Into your hands, O Lord,
We commit ourselves
And all those dear to us this day.
Be with us as we go out and come in.
Strengthen us for the work
That you have given us to do.

after Frank Woods (1874–1932), Bishop of Winchester, England

26 For this new morning and its light,
    For rest and shelter of the night,
    For health and food, love and friends,
    For every gift your goodness sends,
    We thank you, Lord.

    Anonymous

27 Today, Lord,
    Help us to do the things that matter;
    And not to waste the time we are given.
    Fill this day with kindness.
    Amen

28 Good morning God!
    You bring in another day
    Untouched, fresh and new;
    Please help me
    So that this new day will renew me too.
    Take my hand
    And hold it tight
    For I cannot walk alone.
    Amen

    Author unknown

29   Loving God, as we start this day,
Make us happy as we play;
Kind and helpful, being fair,
Letting others have their share.

Anonymous

New Every
Morning

30   Lord,
Here's a fresh, new day
That you have given me,
In which to love you
And help others.
Help me to love you
And do your will.
Amen

31   Lord,

Give me strength to do the right things today,

To make the right choices

And do to others

As I would like them to do to me.

Amen

---

32   We lift our hearts to you, Lord,

And ask you to give us strength for this day.

Be with us in everything we do,

And guide us all the way.

We ask for your help, Lord,

When we stumble and fall.

In your name,

Amen

---

33   Let this day, Lord,

Add some knowledge

Or good deed

To yesterday.

Lancelot Andrewes (1555-1626), Bishop of Winchester,
who looked after the translation of the King James Version of the Bible.

34 Lord,

You know how busy I must be this day.

If I forget you, do not forget me.

Jacob Astley (1579–1652). A general in the English Civil War;
he is said to have used this prayer before battle.

35 Right through this day, Lord,

Let me influence the lives of others for good;

Through the words I speak,

The prayers I say, and the life I live.

Amen

36 Praise the Lord,

Far-off space;

Give thanks to God,

Every home and family.

For God has brought us

to the start of this new day

And he will see us to its end.

Praise God!

Amen

Our Father

37 Our Father in heaven,

May your name be kept holy.

May your kingdom come soon.

May your will be done here on earth,

just as it is in heaven.

Give us our food for today,

and forgive us our sins,

just as we forgive those who sin against us.

And don't let us yield to temptation,

but deliver us from the evil one.

For yours is the kingdom, the power,

and the glory,

Forever and ever,

Amen

The Lord's Prayer, Matthew 6:9–13
Jesus taught this prayer to his disciples when they asked
him to show them how to pray.

38   I love you, my God.
I love you more than anything
   in the world!
Praise to you, God.

Our Father

39   May the eye of God look ahead of me,
The ear of God hear me,
And the word of God speak to me.
Amen

after St Patrick

40   Hello God!
It's me!
What a great day it's been.
Did you see everything I did today?
Of course –
Because you're God!
Thanks for being with me.
Amen

Our Father

41   Almighty God,
     To whom all hearts are open,
     All desires known,
     And from whom no secrets are hid;
     Cleanse the thoughts of our hearts
     By the inspiration of your Holy Spirit,
     That we may perfectly love you,
     And worthily magnify your holy name.
     Through Christ our Lord,
     Amen

from *The Book of Common Prayer*, translated by Thomas Cranmer

42   Keep me safe, O God,
     For in you I take refuge.

Psalm 16:1 NIV

43 O Lord my God,

Give me understanding to know you,

Steadfastness to seek you,

Wisdom to find you,

And faithfulness finally to love you.

Amen

after Thomas Aquinas (1225–74), great Christian thinker

44 Be still!

And know that I am God.

I speak through the storm and clouds.

Be still!

And know that I am God.

Edmond Bordeaux Szekely, adapted

45 Lord,

You are like a shadow of a great rock

in a weary land.

In your endless love

and bottomless care

Bring us to your rest.

after Christina Rossetti (1830–94), English poet

Our Father

46 God of our life,

There are days when the burdens we carry

Make our shoulders ache and weigh us down.

When the road seems dreary and endless,

The sky grey and threatening;

When our lives have no music in them,

And our hearts are lonely.

Flood our path with light, we pray;

Turn our eyes to where the skies are filled

  with promise.

Turn our hearts to brave music.

In the name of Jesus.

Amen

after St Augustine (354–430), great Christian thinker

47 May the hand of God protect me,

The way of God lie ahead of me,

The shield of God defend me

And the love of God save me.

Amen

after Patrick, patron saint of Ireland

Word of God,
Speak to us,
Speak through us,
As you will.

Wisdom of God,
Teach us,
Teach through us,
As you will.

Everlasting truth,
Reveal yourself to us,
So that we may all be taught
  by God.

after Christina Rossetti

Our Father

49   God is our refuge and strength,

A tested help in times of trouble.

Let the oceans roar and foam;

Let the mountains tremble.

There is a river of joy flowing

through the City of our God;

God himself is living in that City.

from Psalm 46 TLB

---

50   Eternal God,

Light of the minds that know you,

Joy of the hearts that love you,

And strength of the wills that serve you;

Grant us so to know you

That we may truly love you;

And so to love you

That we may fully serve you;

Whom to serve is perfect freedom.

St Augustine

51 Dear God,
Did you hear me crying today?
I was sad.
Thank you for listening
When I'm not so happy.

Karen Williamson

52 O God, our help in ages past,
Our hope for years to come,
Be thou our guide while life shall last,
And our eternal home.

Isaac Watts (1674–1748), English hymn writer

53 The light of God surrounds me;
The love of God holds me;
The power of God protects me;
God watches over me.
Wherever I am,
You are, Lord.

Adapted from
James Dillet Freeman's
Prayer for Protection

Our Father

54 Lord, teach me to seek you,

And reveal yourself to me as I look for you.

For I cannot seek you unless you first reach to me,

Nor find you unless you first show yourself to me.

after St Ambrose (c. 340–97), Bishop of Milan

55 Father God

Who in your wisdom

Has ordered our earthly life

So that we need to walk by faith not by sight:

Give us faith so that –

Even when we don't understand what's happening –

We trust in your fatherly care

And are always strengthened by the knowledge

That under us are your everlasting arms.

Anonymous, adapted

Our Daily Bread

56 Thank you for the world so sweet,
Thank you for the food we eat,
Thank you for the birds that sing,
Thank you, God, for everything.

Edith Rutter Leatham

---

57 For all we eat, and all we wear,
For daily bread, and nightly care,
We thank you Heavenly Father.
Amen

---

58 Lord Jesus,
Bless this bread,
As you blessed the boy's five loaves and fishes.
So that all who share it
May have strength and health,
In your name.
Amen

59   God is great, God is good.
     Let us thank him for our food.
     By his hands, we are fed.
     Let us thank him for our bread.
     Amen

Traditional, used by U.S. President, Jimmy Carter

---

60   For health and strength
     and daily food,
     we praise your name,
     O Lord.

Traditional

---

61   Lord,
     Help us share all the good things you give us.
     Bless all those who share this meal with us,
     And bless those who go hungry today,
     Especially little children.
     Amen

62 Our Heavenly Father, kind and good,
we thank you for our daily food.
We thank you for your love and care.
Be with us Lord, and hear our prayer.

63 Heavenly Father,
Help the poor people in the world
Who can't just go to the kitchen and get a biscuit.

64 For what we are about to receive,
may the Lord make us truly thankful.
Amen

Anonymous

65 Tick, Tock!
Hear the clock!
Now it's time to pray.
We fold our hands,
And bow our heads,
And thank the Lord
For our daily bread.

Anonymous

66 Dear God,
We thank you for our food,
for life and joy and play;
We thank you for the special things
you give to us this day.

67 The bread is warm and fresh,
The water cool and clear.
Lord of all life, be with us,
Lord of all life, be near.

African grace

68 Some have meat and cannot eat,
And some want food but lack it.
But we have meat and we can eat
And so the Lord be thanked.

after Robert Burns (1759–96), national poet of Scotland

69 For good food,
and those who prepare it,
for good friends
with whom to share it,
we thank you, Lord.
Amen

DAY BY DAY
Prayers

Our Daily
Bread

70 Loving Father,
We thank you for this food,
And for all your blessings to us.

71 Lord Jesus,
Come and be our guest.
Take your place at this table.
Amen

72 Blessed are you,
Lord our God,
King of Creation,
Who brings bread from the earth.
Amen

Traditional

33

73   Bless, Lord, this food for your use,
and make us always mindful
of the wants and needs of others.
Amen

Traditional

----

74   Lord,
Bless this bunch,
while we munch
our lunch.
Amen

----

75   We thank you, Lord,
for happy hearts,
For rain and sunny weather.
We thank you, Lord,
for this our food,
And that we are together!

76　Dear Jesus,

Thank you for this food.

Bless us all,

And keep us from harm.

Guide and direct us,

Through all our days.

Amen

77　Lord Jesus Christ,

As you blessed many people

with the five loaves and two fishes,

may we too know your blessing

as we share this food;

your peace in our hearts,

and your love in our lives.

Amen

Traditional

78 Father, we thank you for this food,
    For health and strength and all things good.
    May others all these blessings share,
    And hearts be grateful everywhere.

Traditional

79 Lord Jesus Christ, please be our guest,
    And share the food that you have blessed.
    Amen

Traditional

Lord Jesus Christ

80   Christ be with me
and within me;
Christ behind me;
Christ to win me;
Christ to comfort and restore me;
Christ beneath me;
Christ above me;
Christ in quiet and in danger;
Christ in hearts of all that love me;
Christ in mouth of friend and stranger.

This is often called "St Patrick's Breastplate", though probably written after his time. Based on a translation by Mrs C. F. Alexander.

81   Lord Jesus,
Gentle and humble,
Full of mercy and maker of peace,
Help us accept your Good News,
live joyfully by your example,
And inherit your kingdom.
Amen

Anonymous

82   If you can't preach like Peter,
If you can't pray like Paul,
Just tell the love of Jesus,
And say he died for all.

African-American spiritual

83   Dear Lord,
We don't listen properly
To one another.
Teach me to listen
As your son Jesus listened
To everyone who talked to him.
Teach me to be still
So that I may truly hear my brothers and sisters.
Amen

84   Steal away, steal away,
Steal away to Jesus!
Steal away, steal away home,
I ain't got long to stay here.

African-American spiritual

85   Lord Jesus,
Help us
To obey your teaching,
To avoid getting angry,
To increase our love,
And to avoid boastfulness.
In your strength.
Amen

after St Apollonius of Rome (died 185), Christian martyr

86   Jesus, friend of little children,
Be a friend to me;
Take my hand and ever keep me,
Close to thee.

Walter J. Mathams (1853–1931), British hymn writer

Lord Jesus
Christ

87 Dear Lord,
You asked fishermen
on the Sea of Galilee
to follow you.
Help me to follow you too.

see Mark 1:16–20

88 Lord Jesus,
Open our ears and hearts today
To hear your message,
So that through the power
of your death and resurrection
We may walk in newness of life,
As you taught us.
Amen

Hear My Prayer

89   Listen, God, to my prayer!
Please listen and help me.

Psalm 55:1, 2 CEV

90   Every time I feel the spirit
Moving in my heart, I will pray.
Every time I feel the spirit
Moving in my heart, I will pray.

African-American spiritual

91   When I put my hands together,
When I say a prayer,
When I stop and speak your name,
You are there.

Anonymous

92   Bless this house, which is our home:
May we welcome all who come.

Anonymous

93 Lord, I believe;
Help my unbelief.
Lord I am hopeful;
strengthen my hope.
I love you, Lord:
Help me to love you more and more.
In Jesus' name.

Anonymous, adapted

94 Hush little puppy with your bow wow wow,
Hush little kitty with your meow, meow, meow.
Hush Mr Rooster with your cock-a-doodle-doo.
Don't you moo moo moo, Mrs Cow.
Hush, hush, hush.
Hush, hush, hush.
Somebody's talking to God right now.

Traditional

95 Lord,

Be within me to strengthen me,

Outside me to keep,

Over me to shelter,

Beneath me to support,

Before me to direct,

Behind me to restore,

Around me to refresh.

after Lancelot Andrewes

---

96 It's me, it's me, it's me, O Lord,

Standing in the need of prayer;

It's me, it's me, it's me, O Lord,

Standing in the need of prayer.

Not my brother, not my sister, but it's me O Lord,

Standing in the need of prayer;

Not my father, not my mother, but it's me O Lord,

Standing in the need of prayer.

African-American spiritual

97   Lord Jesus Christ,

Friend of sinners,

we thank you for friendship,

Prince of peace,

we ask you that we may be peacemakers.

Amen

Author unknown

---

98   Lord,

Take my heart for your home;

Take my mouth to spread your name;

Take my love and all my strength;

And let my faith never fade.

Amen

after Dwight L. Moody (1837–99), famous American preacher

---

99   All we have is a gift.

It comes, God, from you;

We thank you for it.

100 Lord,

      Help us to remember that

      Love is patient, love is kind.

      It does not boast; it is not proud.

      It is not angry but forgiving.

      Love does not lie.

      It always protects; it always trusts.

      It always hopes; it always tries.

      Love never fails.

      from 1 Corinthians 13

Hear My
Prayer

101 Make me pure, Lord, you are holy;

      Make me meek, Lord: you were lowly.

      Gerard Manley Hopkins (1844–89), English poet

102 For lonely children everywhere,

      Who do not have someone to care.

      Dear God, I pray that you will send

      A loving, kind, and special friend.

      Anonymous

103 This is the church,
And this is the steeple
Open the doors
And see all the people!
Close the doors
And the people all pray.

Traditional

----

104 Dear Lord,
Help my light to shine
so that others will praise you.

based on Matthew 5:16

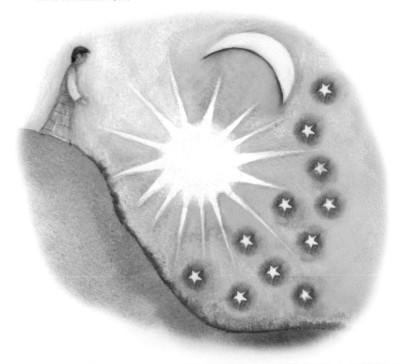

105 Eternal light, shine into our hearts;

Eternal goodness, deliver us from evil;

Eternal Power, be our support;

Eternal Wisdom, scatter our ignorance;

Eternal Pity, have mercy on us.

Amen

after Alcuin of York (c. 735–804), great Christian thinker

---

106 God, make my life a little light

Within the world to glow;

A little flame that burns so bright

Wherever I may go.

Matilda Betham-Edwards (1836–1919), hymn writer and poet

---

107 Father in heaven

hear my prayer.

Keep me in your love and care.

Amen

Traditional

108 **Trinity Prayer**

Love of Jesus, fill us.

Holy Spirit, guide us.

Will of the Father be done.

Amen

109 The things, good Lord, that we pray for,

Give us grace to work for;

Through Jesus Christ,

Amen

Sir Thomas More (1478–1535), adviser to King Henry VIII

110 Dear Lord,

Help me never get tired

of helping others.

based on Galatians 6:9

111 With all that I do,

and all that I say,

help me to walk

in Jesus' way.

Traditional

112 Lord, teach me all that I should know;
In grace and wisdom may I grow.
The more I learn to do your will,
The better may I love you still.

Isaac Watts

113 Lord,
Let my heart –
This sea of restless waves –
Find peace in you.

after St Augustine

114 Bless to me, O God,
The work of my hands.
Bless to me, O God,
The work of my mind.
Bless to me, O God,
The work of my heart.

Anonymous

Hear My
Prayer

115 Dear Lord,
Creator of the world,
Help us to love one another,
Help us to care for one another
As sister or brother.
Bring peace to our world.
Amen

Prayer from Japan

116 May all the happy things we do
Make you, our Father, happy too.
Amen

Anonymous

At the End of School Day

117   Before we go away,
     we bow our heads and pray,
     that God will keep us safe and sound
     until another day.

---

118   Lord we thank you
     Lord we thank you
     Once again
     once again
     And we ask your blessing
     and we ask your blessing
     Ah-ah men,
     Ah-ah men.

     Sung to the tune of Frère Jacques

119 Lord Jesus,
I think about you sometimes,
even when I'm not praying.

120 Lord, help me to do everything
without grumbling or arguing.

from Philippians 2:14

121 Day by day,
Dear Lord, three things I pray:
To see you more clearly,
To love you more dearly,
To follow you more nearly,
Day by day.

Richard de Wych (1197–1253), Bishop of Chichester, England

122 Help us, God, each day,
To follow you along the way.
Teach us to be kind like you,
In everything we say and do.

At the end
of school day

123 Dear God,
I'm glad you love me.
I'm glad you are looking after me.
I feel a lot safer knowing that, Lord.
Amen

Today!

124 Dear Lord Jesus,
We have this day only once.
Before it goes,
help us to do the good we can,
so it's not wasted.
Amen

after Stephen Grellet

---

125 Lord,
Let us not live to be useless,
For Christ's sake.
Amen

John Wesley (1703–91), founder of Methodism

---

126 Dear Jesus,
Please help me at school.
Sometimes I find it hard,
and then I specially need you to help me.
Amen

Karen Williamson

127   Lord, help me love from day to day,
In a helpful sort of way,
To give a smile, lift a load,
For all I meet along life's road.

Anonymous

128   Into your hands, O Lord,
I commit today myself,
My family and friends,
Strangers and enemies.
Help me always
To obey your commands.
Amen

129   Lord, be with us this day.
Within us to purify us;
Above us to draw us up;
Beneath us to sustain us;
Before us to lead us;
Behind us to restrain us;
Around us to protect us.

St Patrick

5

Today!

130 Dear Lord Jesus,
Please help me to be brave.
I'm scared of lots of things.
I'm scared of big boys in the playground.
I'm scared of our friends' dog.
Please take away my fears.
Thank you, God.
Amen

131 Help me, Lord, to remember
That everywhere I am in your presence.
So may all my words and actions
be acceptable in your sight.
Amen

after Susanna Wesley (1669–1742), mother of John Wesley

132 Heavenly Father,
    Open wide the gate into my heart
    So that I may receive your living water
    And be fruitful.

after anonymous Punjabi

Today!

133 Keep my little tongue today,
    Make it kind while I play;
    Keep my hands from doing wrong,
    Guide my feet the whole day long.
    Amen

Author unknown

134 Thank you, Lord, for sleep and rest,
    For all the things that I love best,
    Now guide me through another day.
    Bless my work and bless my play.
    Amen

57

135 God of the city –
   Each street and square –
   Look down on each house
   And bless everyone there.

136 Yesterday I promised
   I'd try to be good today.
   Lord, please help me keep my promise.
   Amen

137 Dear Heavenly Father,
   Help me to guard my words
   whenever I say something.

   Psalm 141:3 CEV

138 Lord Jesus,
Please help me be strong and brave.
Take all my fears away.
Amen

139 We seek your face, Lord;
Turn your face toward us
and show us your glory.
Then shall our longing be satisfied
And our peace be perfect.
Through Jesus Christ our Lord.

140 Dearest Lord,
You are with me,
Your rod and staff comfort me.
When I go on your errands
I know you are – and will be – with me.
How easily you are able to support and refresh
my heart!

after Henry Martyn (1781–1812), English missionary to India

59

141 Thank you, God, for this new day.

In my school, at work and play,

Please be with me all day long,

In every story, game and song.

Author unknown

142 Little deeds of kindness,

Little words of love,

Help to make earth happy,

Like the heaven above.

Julia Carney (1823–1908), American poet

Lead Me Every Step

143 Teach me your ways, O Lord;
Make them known to me.
Teach me to live
According to your truth.

Psalm 25:4–5 GNB

---

144 Lord,
I'm like the man walking to Jericho
who was mugged and left for dead.
Good Samaritan, come and help me.

I'm like the lost sheep.
Good Shepherd,
Seek and find me,
And bring me safe home.
Amen

after St Jerome (c. 347–420), Bible translator

145   Send your light and your truth, Lord,

That we may live always near you.

Let us be ready for every work,

Ready to go out or come in,

To stay or leave,

Just as you decide.

Amen

after Henry Martyn

146   Lord,

Help us often to read your Word

In which there is wisdom and the royal law.

As we read it,

May we increase daily in knowledge of you

And love you with more perfect heart.

Anonymous

147 May God give us:

Light to guide us,

Courage to support us,

Love to unite us,

Now and forever.

Amen

Anonymous

148 O Jesus, I have promised

To serve you to the end,

Please be forever near me

My master and my friend.

I shall not fear the battle

If you are by my side,

Nor wander from the pathway

If you will be my guide.

John E. Bode (1816–74). He wrote this for the
confirmation of his children.

149 Father God,

I am seeking and uncertain.

Watch over each step of mine

And guide me.

after St Augustine

---

150 Peace be in your home

And in your heart,

Or if you roam

Earth's highways wide,

The Lord be at your side,

To bless and guide.

Anonymous

---

151 What will happen to us hereafter we know not;

But to God, who cares for all people,

Who will one day reveal the secrets of all hearts,

We commit ourselves wholly,

And all those near and dear to us.

after Matthew Parker (1504–75), Archbishop of Canterbury

Dear God,

Send the Holy Spirit into my heart.

Teach me,

Guide me,

And direct my thoughts,

From beginning to end.

In your name.

Amen

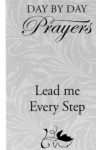

Lead me
Every Step

Lead me
Every Step

153   Guide us, teach us, and strengthen us,

Lord, we ask you,

Until we become as you would have us be:

Pure, gentle, truthful,

Generous, able, and useful;

For your glory.

after Charles Kingsley (1819–75), author of The Water Babies

Lord, Help Me!

154 Please listen, Lord,
and answer my prayer!
I am poor and helpless.
Protect me and save me
because you are my God.

Psalm 86:1–2 CEV

155 Lord,
Make me quick to listen,
Slow to speak,
And slow to get angry.

from James 1:19

156 Lord Jesus,
Thank you for that lady who helped me today.
Help me to help someone else too.

157 In time of difficulty, Lord,
I cannot fight this darkness alone;
Help me to bring the light of Jesus into it.
Amen

based on a prayer from Africa

158 Father,
Let me hold your hand
And like a child walk with you all my days,
Secure in your love and strength.

Thomas à Kempis (c. 1380–1471), author of *The Imitation of Christ*

159 Jesus loves me! – this I know
For the Bible tells me so;
Little ones to him belong –
They are weak, but he is strong.

Anna Bartlett Warner (1827–1915), American writer

160 Dear God,
Thank you that,
with you,
I'm never alone.
Amen

161 Lord, make me an instrument of your peace;

Where there is hatred, let me sow love;

Where there is injury, pardon;

Where there is doubt, faith;

Where there is despair, hope;

Where there is darkness, light;

Where there is sadness, joy.

St Francis of Assisi (c. 1181–1226), known as the patron saint of animals

162 Dear God,

Give us the true courage

That shows itself by gentleness;

Give us the true wisdom

That shows itself by simplicity.

And give us the true power

that shows itself in humility.

after Charles Kingsley

163 Lord,
Never allow us to think
That we can stand by ourselves,
And not need you.

John Donne (1572–1631), English poet and priest

164 Lord,
Help me to know what to do
And what to leave undone.

after Elizabeth Fry (1780–1845), English prison reformer

165 Dear Lord,
You have given me so much;
Give me one more thing
– a grateful heart.

after George Herbert (1593–1633)

166 Lord,
Help me see your glory
In every place.

Michelangelo (1475–1564), Italian painter and sculptor

167 Loving Lord,

Give me a childlike love for you,

Which will cast out all fear.

Edward B. Pusey (1800–82), Oxford professor

Lord, Help
Me!

168 Jesus bids us shine

With a pure, clear light,

Like a little candle

Burning in the night;

In this world of darkness,

So we must shine,

You in your small corner,

And I in mine.

169 Help me, Lord,
carefully watch my temper
And every wrong thought.
Remove anything in me
That may cause another to stumble.

after Christina Rossetti

170 I am trusting you, Lord Jesus;
Never let me fall;
I am trusting you forever,
And for all.

Frances R. Havergal (1836–79), English hymn writer

171 Lord,
Give me a steadfast heart
Which no unfit love may drag down.
Give me an unbeaten heart
That no hardship can wear out.
Give me an upright heart
That no unworthy purpose can tempt.
Amen

after Thomas Aquinas

172 Lord, hear my prayer,

And let my cry come to you.

Do not hide from me in the day of my distress

Turn to me and speedily answer my prayer.

based on Psalm 102:1–2

Lord, Help
Me!

173 Hear my cry, O Lord;

Listen to my prayer.

I call as my heart grows faint.

For you have been my refuge,

a strong tower against my enemy.

from Psalm 61

174 Thank you, God,
For the sun and the trees.
For wonderful flowers
And buzzing bees.

For the sounds I hear
And the sights I see,
But most of all, thank you
For making me me!

175   I know that I am your special child,

and that you love me.

Other children don't know you.

Please may they come to know your love.

I specially pray for… .

Amen

---

176   Lord,

Turning my weeping into joy,

My ignorance into knowledge of your truth,

My fear into love,

My earthly desires into heavenly,

Everything transient into what lasts forever.

Amen

after Thomas à Kempis

177 Lord Jesus,

You are my book,

You are my mirror.

I will turn to you always

To find what I must do.

Help me!

Amen

after Abbé Lasausse, French writer

178 Lord Jesus,

You know how weak I am.

Give me strength

To love you and do your will.

Amen

after St Ephrem the Syrian (c. 306–73), hymn writer

179 Lord,

Grant me the serenity to accept

the things I cannot change,

The courage to change the things I can,

And the wisdom to know the difference.

Amen

attributed to Reinhold Neibuhr

Dear Lord Jesus,
Thank you for loving me.
I love you too.
Amen

181 Lord, I want to be a Christian
in my heart.
Lord, I want to be more loving
in my heart.
Lord, I want to be more holy
in my heart.
Lord, I want to be a Christian
in my heart.

African-American spiritual

182 Lord God,

Help me to live one day at a time,

To enjoy one moment at a time,

To accept hardships as pathway to peace,

to accept this sinful world as it is –

not as I would like to be.

Amen

Author unknown

183 Give thanks to the Lord,

for he is good.

For his mercy lasts forever.

Amen

based on Psalm 107:1

184 Give me love in my heart, Lord Jesus:
Love for you,
Love for those around me,
And love for everyone I find difficult to like.

185 Dear Lord Jesus,
I'm glad that – even if I forget about you –
You will never forget me.

186 Two little eyes to look to God;
Two little ears to hear his word;
Two little feet to walk in his ways;
Two little lips to sing his praise;
Two little hands to do his will
And one little heart to love him still.

Colin C. Kerr

187 Dear God,
Knowing that you love me
makes me feel all warm and happy inside.
Thank you, God.

188 Open my eyes

That I may see

Wonderful things in your law.

Psalm 119:18 NIV

189 The Lord is my shepherd;

I have everything I need.

He lets me rest in fields of green grass

and leads me to quiet pools of fresh water.

Psalm 23:1–2 GNB

190 Give me joy in my heart, keep me praising,

Give me joy in my heart, I pray.

Give me joy in my heart, keep me praising –

Keep me praising till the break of day.

Traditional

191 Lord,

Have mercy on me,

Heal me;

For I have sinned against you.

Psalm 41:4 NIV

192 God be in my head,

And in my understanding;

God be in my eyes,

And in my looking;

God be in my mouth,

And in my speaking;

God be in my heart,

And in my thinking.

from the Sarum Primer (1514)

Lord, Help
Me!

193 Teach me to serve you as you deserve;

To give and not to count the cost;

To fight and not to seek for rest;

To work and not to seek reward

Except to know that I am doing your will.

after St Ignatius of Loyola (1491–1556), founder of the Society of Jesus

194 Lord,

The house of my soul is narrow.

Widen it so you may enter in.

It is in ruins: please repair it!

Who can clean it,

Or who can I call on,

Except you?

Cleanse me from my secret faults, Lord,

And renew my heart.

after St Augustine

195 Lord,

Lead me in the way everlasting.

Psalm 139:24 NRSV

Lord, Help
Me!

196 Use me, my Saviour,

for whatever purpose,

And in whatever way,

you may require.

Here is my poor empty heart:

Fill it with your love.

Here is my sinful, worried soul:

refresh it with your love.

In Jesus' name.

Amen

after Dwight L. Moody

83

Lord, Help
Me!

197 Let my words and my thoughts
Be pleasing to you, Lord,
Because you are my mighty rock
And my protector.

Psalm 19:14 CEV

198 Dear God,
Please help me to tell the truth.
Even if I know it might get me into trouble.
Thank you, Lord.

Others' Sorrows

199 Can I see another's woe,

And not be in sorrow too?

Can I see another's grief,

And not seek for kind relief?

William Blake (1757–1827), English poet and painter

200 Lord Jesus,

I pray for those who are unhappy today:

For children who have no food

For fathers who have no job

For mothers who are sick

For people who are lonely.

Amen

Others'
Sorrows

201 We bring before you, O Lord,

The troubles of people

and the perils of nations,

The sighing of prisoners and captives,

The sorrows of the bereaved,

The needs of strangers,

The helplessness of the weak,

The hopelessness of the weary,

The weakness of the aged.

O Lord, draw near to each of them.

For the sake of Jesus Christ our Lord.

St Anselm (c. 1033–1109), Archbishop of Canterbury

---

202 O Lord,

Release all who are in trouble,

For you are our God,

Who sets captives free;

Who gives hope to the hopeless;

Who lifts up the fallen;

And who is the safe haven of the shipwrecked.

from the Liturgy of St Mark

203 Dear God,

Thank you that I have a nice home.

Not everyone does.

Thank you that I have family around me.

Not everyone does.

Thank you that I have toys and games.

Not everyone does.

Please look after all the children who go without.

Amen

204 Lord, please help me notice

When people need a hand.

Help me notice when they are sad

And need a friend.

Don't let me get so busy

That I don't see

When someone needs

A bit of help from someone like me.

205 Lord,

We are your people,

The sheep of your flock.

Heal the sheep that are wounded,

Comfort the sheep that are in pain,

Warm the sheep that are cold,

Calm the sheep that are fearful.

In your name.

Amen

------

206 Father of the poor,

Lord of the weak,

Help us to take the side of the poor,

To defend newcomers,

To welcome the stranger,

To befriend the friendless.

Bring us together in peace, justice, and love.

Amen

207 Lord Jesus,

Friend of the friendless,

Help me with those who are difficult to love.

Strengthen me when they criticize

And point the finger;

When they ignore me

And turn their backs.

Help me to see them

In the light of your love.

Amen

Others'
Sorrows

The People I Love

208   Lord,
      Bless our family,
      Protect and bless us –
      Present or absent –
      At home or away.
      Amen

209   God bless all those I love;
      God bless all those who love me;
      God bless all those who love those I love,
      And all those who love those who love me.

      from an old New England sampler

210   Lord Jesus,
      Thank you for Gran and Grandad
      Please look after them as they grow older.
      Amen

90

211 Dear God,
I'm glad you love Daddy and Mummy
and me and everybody.
I want to love you, too,
and grow up to be strong and good.
Amen

212 Lord,
We thank you for being with each of us today,
while we were apart, and for being with us tonight.
Help us to remember those
who have so much less than we do.
Bless us as a family.
Help us to grow in love and care for each other.
We ask you to comfort and give strength and peace
to those who are sick or struggling in any way.
Lord, be with us today.

213 Lord,

Thank you for those in my life

Who are easy to love.

I thank you for family and friends

Who support me

And who comfort me in difficult times.

Amen

214 Dear Lord Jesus,

When you were a child living on earth,

you always obeyed your parents.

Please help me to do the same.

Thank you.

215 Lord God,

Our Heavenly Father,

Thank you for my mum and dad,

And for our home.

Bless us all,

And help us to love you.

Amen

216 Thank you, Lord,

for the gift of my family.

Be with us in our good times

and in our sad and difficult times.

Help us always remember

our love for one another.

In the name of Jesus.

Amen

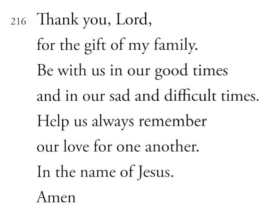

217 Dear God,
Bless this family,
As we begin a new school year.
Let our home be a place to learn forgiveness,
Love, and co-operation.
Through Jesus Christ.
Amen

Anonymous

218 Our Heavenly Father,
Thank you for my dad.
Help me know how much he loves me.
Give him a healthy body,
A successful life,
And a peaceful soul.
Amen

219 Dear God,
Thank you so much for my family.
Please look after all the lonely children
    everywhere, Lord.
Amen

220   Dear Father in heaven,
Look down from above;
Bless father and mother
And all whom I love.

Anonymous

221   Lord,
Protect our family
From all evil.
Keep us together
In the love of Christ.
Amen

222   For health and food,
For love and friends,
For everything your goodness sends,
Father in heaven, we thank you.
Amen

223   God let our home be friendly,
With open doors to all
Who come for food and shelter,
Or just to pay a call.

The People
I Love

224 Father God,
Thank you for my family –
not just those who live here,
but grandparents, uncles, aunties, and cousins.
Please be with all of them today.
Amen

225 Dear God,
Please love me,
Take care of me,
Bless me.

Please love my sister,
Take care of her,
Bless her.

Please love my brother,
Take care of him,
Bless him.
Amen

Karen Williamson

226 Peace be to this house
And to all who dwell here.
Peace be to those who enter
And to those who depart.

Anonymous

227 Lord Jesus,
My friend moved last week.
I miss her and she misses me.
Help us both find new friends
So we stop feeling sad.

The People
I Love

228 Loving Heavenly Father,
　　　 Bless our family.
　　　 Guard us from all harm;
　　　 deliver us from anger and envy.
　　　 In the name of Jesus.
　　　 Amen

---

229 Dear Lord,
　　　 Help me to see when people need my help.
　　　 Children who don't have friends,
　　　 My parents and teachers,
　　　 When they need a hand.
　　　 Amen

I'm So Sorry!

230   Dear God,
We're sorry for doing wrong things.
Please forgive us.
Help us forgive people
Who are unkind to us.
Amen

231   God, you are great.
You made the world – and it's good.
Thank you for making it so beautiful.
We're sorry we've spoiled it.
Amen

Karen Williamson

232   Dear Father God,
Forgive me for doing wrong.
And help me to forgive others.

based on Matthew 6:14

233 Dear God,
I did something wrong today.
You know what it was, Lord.
I'm sorry.
Please forgive me.
Thank you, God.

234 Lord,
I'm sorry for my bad mood today.
I'm glad that – whether I'm good or bad –
You love me anyway.

235 Although I'm full of fear
and feel I've failed,
I cry to you, Lord.
Hear my voice.
For you are full of mercy
And will forgive us all.
May your mercy come
As certain as new dawn.
Amen

Traditional

236 Lord,

If during today I have done wrong,

In word or deed or thought,

Forgive me.

For you are full of goodness and mercy.

Give me peaceful, undisturbed sleep

And wake me tomorrow for another day.

Amen

Traditional

I'm So Sorry!

237 For the things that I've done wrong,

Things that I remember long,

Hurting friends and those I love,

I'm very sorry, God.

Anonymous

I'm So Sorry!

238   Dear Lord,
We confess our sins and shortcomings.
Blot out our wrongdoing.
Give us a new and steadfast spirit.
Restore us to friendship with you.
Amen

239   You can build your prayer around four themes:
Thanks, Sorry, Please, and I love you.

We thank God for being there and for all he has
given us.
We are sorry for our faults.
We see that we are poor and ask him for what we need.
We feel loved and love him in return.

What a Wonderful World!

240 Praise God, from whom all blessings flow.

Praise him all creatures here below.

Praise him above, angelic host,

Praise Father, Son, and Holy Ghost.

Thomas Ken (1637–1711), Bishop of Bath & Wells, England

241 Dear Father God,

Thank you for giving us a special time

To tell you that we love you.

Help us feel you in our hearts,

So that we know you are here with us.

In Jesus' name we pray.

Amen

What a
Wonderful
World!

242 For the beauty of the earth,

For the beauty of the skies,

For the love which from our birth

Over and around us lies.

Lord of all, to you we raise

This our grateful song of praise.

after Folliott S. Pierpoint (1835–1917), English schoolmaster

243 Merciful Father,

I thank you from the bottom of my heart

That you heard my prayer

And answered it

In your endless mercy.

Amen

244 God bless the animals,

Great and small,

And help us to learn

To love them all.

245 O God! Who gives the winter's cold,
　　　As well as summer's joyous rays,
　　　Us warmly in your love enfold,
　　　And keep us through life's wintry days.

Samuel Longfellow 1819–92, adapted

246 Dear Lord Jesus,
　　　We had a big storm today.
　　　There was thunder and lightning,
　　　Crashing and banging!
　　　I felt frightened.
　　　I wanted to run away and hide.
　　　Please help me not to be so afraid.
　　　Thank you, God.
　　　Amen

247 Dear God,

Thank you for the clothes I'm wearing today.

Please send joy into the lives

Of the people who made them

And all the other good things

In my life.

Help us to love one another

As you have loved us.

Amen

248 Lord,

Thank you for the many times you helped me,

Always hearing when I called.

You always listen and have pity;

You always come to help us.

You change our weeping to dancing;

You always fill us with joy.

after Psalm 30

Bless us all!

249 Lord,
Lift up the light of your face upon us
So that in your light we may see light.

after Lancelot Andrewes

---

250 May the grace of the Lord Jesus Christ,
And the love of God,
And the fellowship of the Holy Spirit,
Be with you all.

2 Corinthians 13:14 NIV

Bless us all!

251 May the Lord bless us,

And keep us from evil,

And bring us to everlasting life.

Amen

from the Sarum Primer

252 Give peace in our time, O Lord.

Because there is no one else

who fights for us,

but only you, O God.

adapted from *The Book of Common Prayer*

253 The Lord bless us and keep us.

The Lord make his face to shine upon us,

And be gracious to us,

And give us peace,

Both now and evermore.

Amen

based on Numbers 6:24–27

The Earth is Full of Your Riches

254 All things bright and beautiful,
All creatures great and small,
All things wise and wonderful,
The Lord God made them all.

He gave us eyes to see them,
And lips that we might tell,
How great is God Almighty,
Who has made all things well.

Mrs C. F. Alexander (1818–95), Irish hymn writer and poet

255 God,
The source and giver of everything,
For the sun and rain,
the overflowing fruit of the trees,
and crops of our fields,
We thank you.

256 Our Heavenly Father,
Help us to see all animals as gifts from you,
And to treat them with respect.
We pray for all animals that are suffering
Because we have neglected them.
Amen

after St Francis of Assisi

----

257 Lord,
Thank you for the pleasure
you give me through my senses.
I thank you for the delight of colour,
The awe of sunset,
The wild flowers in the hedges,
The smile of friendship.
Truly, Lord, the earth is full of your riches.

after Edward King (1829–1910), English bishop

258 Thank you for cows that give us milk,
and hens that lay eggs.
Thank you for all the farm animals.
Amen

259 Lord,
Creator of all life,
Help us to see afresh
The miracle of life,
And the value of all living things.
Help us protect life,
In your name.
Amen

260 For flowers that bloom about our feet,
Father we thank you.
For tender grass so fresh, so sweet,
Father we thank you.

For birdsong and hum of bee,
For all things fair we hear or see,
Father in heaven, we thank you.

The Earth
is Full of your
Riches

261 God, who made the earth,
The air, the sky, the sea,
Who gave the light its birth,
Careth for me.

God, who made the grass,
The flower, the fruit, the tree,
The day and night to pass,
Careth for me.

Sarah B. Rhodes (1829–1904)

---

262 For air and sunshine, pure and sweet,
We thank our Heavenly Father;
For grass that grows beneath our feet,
We thank our Heavenly Father.

For lovely flowers and blossoms gay,
For trees and woods in bright array,
For birds that sing in joyful lay,
We thank you, Heavenly Father.

Anonymous

263 Thank you, Lord Jesus,
For all the plants and animals
You've given us to share –
From the yellow daffodil,
To the grizzly bear.

Karen Williamson

The Earth
is Full of your
Riches

264 Dear Father, hear and bless
Your beasts and singing birds;
And guard with tenderness
Small things that have no words.

Author unknown

265 The rainbow high above us
So colourful and free;
When we look upon it
It's God's love we see.

---

266 Dear Lord,
Today we went to the zoo.
We saw lots of animals you made.
Giant elephants, teeny lizards,
Chattering monkeys, gentle deer,
Waddling penguins, roaring lions.
You made them all, God,
Big and small.

267 Thank you, God,

For cats and dogs,

For lions, and bears, and tigers,

For kangaroos, and rhinos,

And for the birds that sing.

Amen

The Earth
is Full of your
Riches

268 Dear Lord in heaven,

Look on our sowing:

Bless the little gardens

And the green things growing.

Anonymous

269 Lord,

You let animals be near you at your birth.

Teach us to be kind to all animals;

Always caring for our pets,

And never harming any creature

That you put upon your earth.

Amen

270 Thank you, God, for rain
and beautiful rainbow colours.
Thank you for letting us
splash in the puddles.

Author unknown

271 Thank you for the beasts so tall
Thank you for the creatures small.
Thank you for all things that live
Thank you, God, for all you give.

272 Thank you for making the sun, moon, and stars,
And the earth, and planets, and comets.
It's all so huge and amazing, Lord.

273 Lord,
Thank you that we can sing to you.
Because music is such fun,
and we sing such great songs.
Amen

274 **Thank you for the seasons, Lord**

Thank you for spring,
When lambs are born
And flowers bloom.

Thank you for long, hot, summer days,
When we can play outside
And enjoy the sunshine.

Thank you for autumn,
When fruit is ripe for picking,
And golden leaves tumble from trees.

And thank you for winter,
With its ice and snow.

275 Dear God,
From whom comes every good and perfect gift;
Accept our thanks
And give us health.
That we may evermore
Serve you with all our strength and might.
Amen

after John Cosin (1594–1672), Bishop of Durham

Health and Healing

276   Loving Father,
We pray for all those who heal the sick
And prevent disease and illness.
Give them wisdom and strength
As they work to help others.
Amen

277   Lord God,
We place our worries in your hands.
We trust the sick to your care,
And ask that you restore them
To full health.
Amen

278 Dear Lord,
Watch with those who wake,
Or watch,
Or work,
Or weep tonight.
Protect those who sleep.
Amen

after St Augustine

279 O Lord,
You are the only source
Of health and healing.
Help me feel you with me,
And give me health, strength, and peace.
Through Jesus Christ,
Amen

280 Lord Jesus,
Please make my friend well.
Help the doctors and nurses
Make her better.
Amen

Karen Williamson

Health and
Healing

281 Dear Lord,

When you lived on this earth,

you healed the sick and diseased.

May your healing hand rest on me

And restore me to full health.

Amen

282 Loving Father,

I trust myself to your care today.

Please restore me to full health.

Into your hands I commend myself.

Amen

283 Merciful Father,

Comfort all who are sick or distressed.

Turn their thoughts to you,

So that they may serve you

And bring forth good fruit.

284 Care for your sick ones,

Lord Jesus;

Rest your tired ones;

Bless your dying ones;

Comfort your suffering;

Protect the joyful.

All for your name's sake.

Amen

after St Augustine

Health and
Healing

On Our Travels

285   Dear Lord,
Bless this journey I have to take.
May I reach its end safe and sound;
And return to my family
In good health.
Amen

286   Heavenly Father,
Be with us as we travel.
Keep us safe every mile of the way.
Make us cautious, careful, and
concerned travellers.
Keep our roads safe and free from danger.
Amen

287 **For Those at Sea**

Almighty, everlasting Father,

Protector of all those who put their trust in you:

Hear our prayer for those who sail the seas.

Give them courage

And bring them safe to their destination.

Bless all their loved ones,

wherever they may be.

Amen

288 Lord Jesus,

Protect us from all perils and dangers,

As we travel.

Defend us from any accident,

So that we arrive safely.

We put our trust and hope in you,

Now and forever.

Amen

Extra-special Days

Christmas

289 Away in a manger,
No crib for a bed.
The little Lord Jesus
Laid down his sweet head.

The stars in the bright sky
Looked down where he lay;
The little Lord Jesus
Asleep in the hay.

Author unknown

290 What can I give him,
Poor as I am?
If I were a shepherd,
I would give a lamb;
If I were a wise man,
I would do my part;
Yet what I can I give him –
Give my heart.

Christina Rossetti

124

291 May Christmas morning make us happy
to be your children.
And Christmas evening bring us to our beds
with grateful thoughts.
For Jesus' sake.

Robert Louis Stevenson (1850–94), Scottish author and poet

292 Happy birthday, Jesus!

Thank you for sharing this special day with us!

The wise men brought gifts,

So we give presents.

Your family was happy,

So we have parties and food.

Happy birthday, Jesus!

---

293 Loving Father,

Help us remember the birth of Jesus,

That we may share in the song of the angels,

The gladness of the shepherds,

And the worship of the wise men.

Robert Louis Stevenson

---

294 Joy to the world!

The Lord is come.

Let earth receive her King.

Let every heart

Prepare him room,

And heaven and nature sing.

Isaac Watts

295 Lord Jesus,

Wise men journeyed for miles

to bring you the first Christmas presents.

So may we, too, remember with thankful hearts

the love that comes with each present we open.

We also thank you for the love

you have for each of us,

and we thank you for the many gifts

that you give us.

Amen

296 Go, tell it on the mountain,

Over the hills and everywhere;

Go tell it on the mountain

That Jesus Christ is born.

African-American spiritual

---

297 Close the door of hate,

and open the door of love,

all over the world.

Let kindness come with every gift,

and good wishes with every greeting.

Deliver us from evil

by the blessing Christ brings.

And teach us to be merry with clear hearts.

Robert Louis Stevenson

298 **At Christmas dinner**

We thank you, Father God,
for the love that binds us,
for the food that nourishes us,
and for giving your Son
into our world to save us.
Amen

New Year

299 For each new year,
And everything it brings,
We give you thanks,
O Lord.

300 Lord,
A new year is beginning.
Help us face this year with the will to do good.
Help us make this world a better place,
now and forever.
Amen

Easter

301 There is a green hill far away,
Outside a city wall,
Where the dear Lord was crucified,
Who died to save us all.

Mrs C. F. Alexander

302 Jesus Christ is risen today.
Alleluia!

303 Easter eggs! Easter eggs!
Give to him that begs!
For Christ the Lord is risen.

To the poor, open door,
Something give from your store!
For Christ the Lord is risen.

Those who love freely give,
Long and well may they live!
For Christ the Lord is risen.

Traditional Russian Easter song

Harvest

304　All good gifts around us
　　Are sent from heaven above.
　　Then thank the Lord,
　　O thank the Lord,
　　For all his love.

Matthias Claudius (1740–1815), German poet
Translated by Jane Montgomery Campbell (1817–78)

305　First the seed
　　And then the grain;
　　Thank you, God,
　　For sun and rain.

　　Thank you, God,
　　For all your care;
　　Help us all
　　To give and share.

306   Now thank we all our God
With hearts and hands and voices;
Such wonders he has done
In him his world rejoices.

Martin Rinkart (1586–1649), German clergyman and hymn writer
Translated by Catherine Winkworth (1827–78)

307   First the blade and then the ear,
Then the full corn shall appear.
Lord of the harvest, grant that we
Wholesome grain and pure may be.

Henry Alford (1810–71), English writer

Sunday

308 This is the day that the Lord has made;
We will rejoice and be glad in it.

based on Psalm 118:24

Birthdays

309 Thank you, Lord,
for people and parties,
For presents and cards,
For songs and games.
Thank you, Lord,
for cakes and candles.
Thank you for birthdays, Lord.

Karen Williamson

310 Today it's my birthday!
Please give me a happy day –
and all the other children born today.

Holidays

311 Thank you, God, for holidays –
For summer clothes and summer play –
And sunny, summer days.

312 Dear Lord,
Thank you for holidays,
And all the fun we have.
Thank you for the people who take us.
Amen

313 Dear Lord,
I'm glad that, when we are far from home,
you are still with us.
Please keep us safe.
Amen

Thank You So Much!

314   Lord Jesus,
      Thank you for my friends,
      and for the games and fun we share.
      Please help me to be a good friend to them.
      Amen

315   For food, and clothes, and toys, and such,
      We thank you, Lord, so very much.
      Amen

316   We give thanks for our bread,
      We give thanks for our butter,
      And most of all,
      We give thanks for each other.
      Amen

      Traditional

Thank you
so much!

317 Hello God!

I saw so many people today.

My best friend.

My teacher.

My brother and sister.

Mum and Dad.

The lady next door.

Thanks for all the great people in my day.

Amen

318 For the birds and the trees
and the sounds of the leaves,
For all that we have,
thank you God.

Thank you
so much!

319 **A page of thank yous**

Sun
Rain
Beautiful flowers
Cats
Tall trees
Twisting rivers
Wiggly worms
Bright leaves
Orangey sunsets
Dogs
Peacocks
Daffodils
For food, for friends,
For all God sends.
We give our thanks to you.
Amen

Day is Done

320 Dear God,
I love bath time.
I have lots and lots of bubbles.
I pretend I'm swimming in the sea.
It's such fun.
Thank you for my bath time.

---

321 Father God,
When Mum turns off the light,
please be with me.
Help me to get to sleep,
and please give me good dreams.
Amen

322 Hello God!
Did you hear me laughing today?
It was so funny.
Thank you for giving us so much fun.
Amen

323 Day is done.
Gone the sun,
From the lake,
From the hills,
From the sky.
All is well,
safely rest.
God is near.

Anonymous

324 Lord Jesus,
Let my near and dear ones be
Always near and dear to you.
Bring me, and all those I love,
To your happy home above.

Frances R. Havergal

325   Bless us in the morning,
Bless us through the day,
Bless us as we go to sleep,
And keep us safe, we pray.

326   Help me not to worry about tomorrow.
You have told us
it will look after itself.

from Matthew 6:34

327   God our Father, I come to say,
Thank you for your love today.
Thank you for my family,
And all the friends you give to me.
Amen

328 Lord Jesus,

Thank you for everything good that happened today:

For keeping me safe and well,

For fun with friends,

For what I learned,

For those I love.

Help me to sleep safely tonight.

Amen

Karen Williamson

329 Dear God, I thank you every time I pray:

For keeping me safe all through the day.

For blessing me with your love and care,

For teaching me to give and share.

Bless my friends, and bless me, too,

In everything I say and do.

Author unknown

330 Now the light has gone away;

Jesus, listen while I pray.

Asking you to watch and keep

And to send me quiet sleep.

Frances R. Havergal

331 Jesus, tender Shepherd, hear me:
Bless your little child tonight;
Through the darkness, please be near me,
Keep me safe till morning light.

All this day your hand has led me,
Now I thank you for your care;
You have warmed me, clothed and fed me;
Listen to my evening prayer.

Mary L. Duncan (1814–40), Scottish hymn writer

332 Lord, keep us safe this night,
     Secure from all our fears;
     May angels guard us while we sleep,
     Till morning light appears.

John Leland (1754–1841), American opponent of slavery

----

333 I see the moon,
     And the moon sees me;
     God bless the moon,
     And God bless me.

Traditional

----

334 May the Lord support us all the long day,
     Till the shadows lengthen
     And the evening comes.
     Till the busy world is hushed
     And the busyness of life is over,
     The work is done.
     In your mercy,
     Bring us safe home at last,
     To your holy rest and peace.

after John Henry Newman, English hymn writer

335 Before I close my eyes tonight,
I thank you, Lord, with all my might
For my friends and family, too,
And everyone who's at my school.

Anonymous

336 Heavenly Father,
As this day ends
Bless me for I am tired.
Help me to turn to you,
For I need you.
Amen

337 Now the day is over,
Night is drawing nigh;
Shadows of the evening
Steal across the sky.

Jesus, give the weary
Calm and sweet repose;
With your tenderest blessing,
May our eyelids close.

Sabine Baring-Gould (1834–1924), who wrote more than 1200 works

Day is Done

338   Hello God!

I'm thinking about tomorrow.

It's a new day.

Help me do something special

And something kind.

339   Now I lay me down to sleep,

I pray the Lord your child to keep.

Your love guard me through the night,

And wake me with the morning light.

Traditional

340   Be near me, Lord Jesus!

I ask you to stay

Close by me forever

And love me, I pray.

Bless all the dear children

In Thy tender care

And take us to heaven

To live with you there.

341 Jesus, Saviour, wash away
All that has been wrong today:
Help me every day to be
Good and gentle, more like you.

Frances R. Havergal

---

342 Dear God,
Tomorrow is a very important day for me.
You know about it already.
Please look after me tomorrow.
Thank you for listening, God.
I'm not so worried now.

---

343 Soft moonbeams light the garden,
The sky is starry bright,
Dear Father up in heaven,
Please bless us all tonight.

344 Gentle Jesus, hear me,
Will you please be near me,
I don't want to be alone,
Feeling sad all on my own.

Tomorrow will be different –
It's the start of a new day,
But until the morning comes,
Stay close to me, I pray.

Day is Done

149

As We Sleep

345   Goodnight! Goodnight!
Far flies the light;
But still God's love
Shall flame above,
Making all bright.
Goodnight! Goodnight!

Victor Hugo (1802–85), French writer, author of *Les Miserables*

346   The moon shines bright,
The stars give light
Before the break of day.

God bless you all,
Both great and small,
And send a joyful day.

Traditional

As We Sleep

347 Hush, my dear, lie still and slumber.
Holy angels guard your bed!
Heavenly blessings without number
Gently fall upon your head.

Isaac Watts

348 Loving shepherd of your sheep,
Keep your lamb, in safety keep;
Nothing can your power withstand,
None can take me from your hand.

Jane Eliza Leeson (1808–81), English hymn writer

349 Be our light in the darkness, Lord,
and in your great mercy
defend us from all perils and dangers of this night.
For the love of your only son,
our Saviour Jesus Christ.
Amen

from *The Book of Common Prayer*

350 Dear God,

Please look after me at bedtime.

Sometimes I wake up in the middle of the night
   and feel scared.

Help me remember that you are always with me –

Then I won't need to be afraid.

Day and night, God,

I'm glad you're my friend.

351 We give thanks to you, Heavenly Father,

Through Jesus Christ, your dear Son,

That you have this day protected us by your grace.

We ask you to forgive us all our sins

And the wrong we have done.

By your great mercy defend us

From all the perils and dangers of this night.

Into your hands we commend ourselves,

And all that is ours.

Amen

after Martin Luther (1483–1546), German religious reformer

352 As night-time comes creeping,
And children are sleeping,
God watches us, deep through the night.

So hush now, no peeping,
For God will be keeping
Us safe, till the new morning's light.

353 Sleep my child, and peace attend you,
All through the night;
Guardian angels God will send you,
All through the night.

Traditional, Welsh

354 I will not fear
For God is near,
Through the dark night
As in the light.
And while I sleep,
Safe watch does keep.
Why should I fear,
When God is near?

355   Through the night your angels kept
Watch round me while I slept;
Now the dark has gone away
Lord, I thank you for the day.

after William Canton

356   When the sun has said goodbye,
And little stars shine in the sky,
You're still with me, not far above,
Right in my heart, for you are Love.

357   Dear Jesus,
As a hen covers her chicks with her wings
To keep them safe,
We pray that this night you protect us
Beneath your golden wings.

Anonymous, Indian

358   Matthew, Mark, Luke, and John,
Bless the bed that I lie on.
Four angels to my bed,
Four angels round my head.

Traditional

359 I pray whatever wrongs I've done,
You will forgive me every one.
Be near me when I wake again,
And bless all of those I love.
Amen

Traditional

360 The peace of all peace
be mine this night.
In the name of the Father,
And of the Son,
And of the Holy Spirit.
Amen

Celtic prayer

361 Be with us, Lord,

and protect us through the hours of this night,

so we who are wearied

by the changes and

chances of this life

may rest in your eternal changelessness.

Amen

adapted from *The Book of Common Prayer*

362 From ghoulies and ghosties,

Long-legged beasties,

And things that go bump in the night,

Good Lord deliver us!

Traditional Cornish prayer

363 Keep me as the apple of your eye;

Hide me in the shadow of your wings.

Lighten my darkness, Lord.

May the light of your presence

Drive away the shadows of night.

Amen

adapted from the Boisil Compline

364   Lord, keep your people

in your protecting arms.

Shelter them under your wings.

Be their light in darkness.

Be their hope in sadness.

Be their calm in worry.

Be strength in their weakness.

Be their comfort in pain.

Be their song in the night.

Amen

Celtic prayer

365   O Lord,

Watch over all who sleep tonight.

Tend the sick, rest the weary.

May we wake safely in the morning

to start a new day.

For your love's sake.

Amen

Subject Index

Please note that the number after each entry is the prayer number.

Authors

Please note that the number after each entry is the prayer number.